Euthanasia and the "Right to Die"

A Pro/Con Issue

Renée C. Rebman

HOT
PRO/CON
ISSUES

Enslow Publishers, Inc.
40 Industrial Road   PO Box 38
Box 398   Aldershot
Berkeley Heights, NJ 07922   Hants GU12 6BP
USA   UK
http://www.enslow.com

Library of Congress Cataloging-in-Publication Data

Rebman, Renée C., 1961–
    Euthanasia and the "right to die" : a pro/con issue / Renée C.
Rebman.
       p. cm.
    Includes bibliographical references and index.
    ISBN 0-7660-1816-4
    1. Euthanasia—Juvenile literature. 2. Right to die—Juvenile lit-
erature. [1. Euthanasia. 2. Right to die.] I. Title.
    R726 .R42 2001
    179.7—dc21

                      2001005251

Printed in the United States of America

10 9 8 7 6 5 4 3 2 1

To Our Readers:
We have done our best to make sure all Internet Addresses in this book
were active and appropriate when we went to press. However, the author
and the publisher have no control over and assume no liability for the
material available on those Internet sites or on other Web sites they may
link to. Any comments or suggestions can be sent by e-mail to com-
ments@enslow.com or to the address on the back cover.

Illustration Credits: All photos are by AP/Wide World Photos,
except for the following: Enslow Publishers, Inc., p. 27.

Cover Illustration: AP/Wide World Photos. Shown are demon-
strators in the state of Oregon, where voters had to decide if a
state law allowing terminally ill adults to obtain lethal drugs from
a physician should be repealed or retained. The majority voted
"No" to the repeal, and Oregon kept the law allowing lethal prescriptions.

Contents

Chapter 1

What Is a Good Death?

Eli Kahn, a seventy-eight-year-old man, was admitted to the hospital in poor health. He wanted to be left alone to die. He felt his time had come to leave the earth. He did not want to be connected to machines to continue living. In his own words, Kahn expressed his feelings: "The engine is broken down, it is time for the engineer to abandon it."

His wishes were not followed. Instead, he was connected to a mechanical respirator, which kept him breathing. During the night, Kahn woke up and somehow managed to reach over and switch off the machine. Before he died, he wrote this message: "Death is not the enemy, doctor. Inhumanity is."[1]

Eli Kahn's story raises many questions. Was it humane for the doctor to try to prolong Kahn's life when Kahn was clearly ready to die? Was it legal to put him on a respirator against his will? Do we have the right to die? Is it immoral to choose the time of our own death? Should it be legal for medical doctors to assist in causing death if the patient requests it? These questions, and many others, fuel the controversy over the subject of euthanasia.

"Good Death"

The term *euthanasia* is taken from the Greek language. *Eu* means "good" and *thanatos* means "death"; euthanasia means "good death." Euthanasia is also referred to as mercy killing or assisted suicide. (It is also used to refer to the killing of very ill or injured animals.)

Euthanasia involves allowing someone to die or even helping him or her to die. This practice has been accepted in some societies, while others

*T*here are active people on both sides of the debate over euthanasia. Here, a group collects signatures to put a law permitting physician-assisted suicide on the ballot in Michigan.

strongly reject it. Religious beliefs, ethical standards, and legal battles all play a part in modern debates on euthanasia. Modern technology has given us the means to prolong life. But it is not always able to ensure the quality of life. Many people with incurable illnesses suffer long periods of intense pain. When they wish to end that pain through death, society often does not accept that decision.

Types of Euthanasia

Active euthanasia means causing the death of a person through a direct action. This is often done by a lethal injection of drugs. When the drugs are given by a doctor, it is called physician-assisted suicide. Passive euthanasia means denying or withdrawing artificial means of prolonging life in order to let nature take its course.

Involuntary euthanasia is euthanasia committed against a person's wishes. Involuntary euthanasia is considered murder.

The debate over euthanasia involves the question of giving people choices at the end of life. For example, should they be allowed to refuse treatment or request lethal drugs? How much control should a person have over his or her own body? By law, this control is limited. In fact, active euthanasia is currently legal only in the Netherlands, Japan, Colombia, and the state of Oregon.

Opposition to euthanasia is widespread. It often comes from religious groups who find euthanasia to be immoral. Many people feel euthanasia is merely a form of suicide, which they believe is a sin. They feel that God gives life and that only God can take it away.

Groups concerned with disabilities are frequently

opposed to euthanasia. They ask, Is euthanasia the first step toward a world in which disabled people can be disposed of against their will?

The Hippocratic Oath

Much of the medical profession is also opposed to euthanasia. They believe their job is to keep people alive, not to let life end or to help patients die. In fact, doctors take a pledge known as the Hippocratic Oath that specifically forbids active euthanasia:

> I will use treatment to help the sick according to my ability and judgment, but never with a view to injury and wrongdoing. Neither will I administer a poison to anybody when asked to do so, nor will I suggest such a course.[2]

The "Slippery Slope" Argument

The "slippery slope" argument is a term used in many philosophical discussions that has become a catchphrase in the controversy over euthanasia. The basic idea behind this type of argument is that if society takes the first step in the wrong direction (down the slope), then it inevitably ends up in the worst possible situation (at the bottom). In the case of euthanasia, people argue that if it were legalized, it would lead to a general decline in respect for human life. Opponents of euthanasia fear that many lives would be in jeopardy if this step were taken. They believe that a general acceptance of euthanasia in society would lead to mercy killings of those in intense pain as well as the disabled, the elderly, and the poor. In short, they believe that active euthanasia would lead to involuntary euthanasia.

Barney Clark's Key

At sixty-one, Barney Clark was dying from heart disease. On December 21, 1982, the retired dentist became the first person to receive an artificial heart. After the transplant, Clark was hooked up to a compressor by two six-foot hoses. This compressor was essential to keep him alive.

Before the surgery, Clark had signed a consent form that stated:

> I understand I am free at any time to withdraw my consent to participate in this experimental project, recognizing that the exercise of such an option after the artificial heart is in place may result in my death.

Clark was given a special key. He could use it to turn off the compressor if he no longer wanted to live tied to the machine.

Dr. William Kolft, the founder of the artificial heart program, agreed with this option:

> I think it is entirely legitimate that this man whose life has been extended should have the right to cut it off if he doesn't want it, if life ceases to be enjoyable. The operation won't be a success unless he is happy.

Clark had an option of euthanasia that is denied to many other patients.

Barney Clark never used his key. He died sixteen weeks after the operation. But the choice he was given is what proponents of euthanasia want for those with dire medical problems.[3]

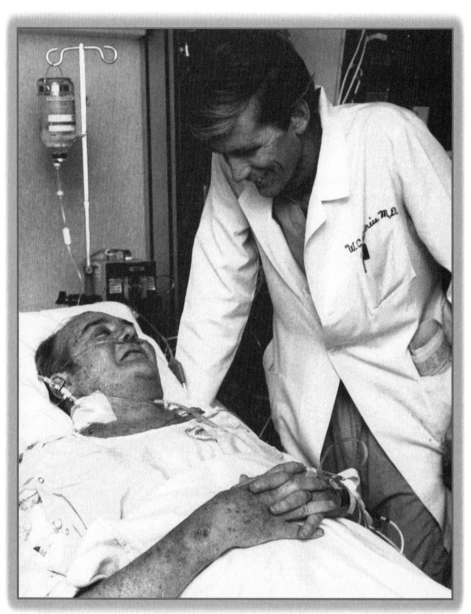

*B*arney Clark, the first recipient of an artificial heart, lived for 112 days after it was implanted. He was granted the option of turning off the machines that kept him alive. Above, he smiles at his surgeon, Dr. William DeVries.

Tactics

Unfortunately, groups on either side of the euthanasia debate often use scare tactics, exaggerated statistics, and slanted articles to support their points. For example, groups for euthanasia often describe horrendous cases of terminally ill patients in unrelenting pain, even though that is not the norm.

Those against euthanasia claim that physician-assisted euthanasia is not always requested by the patient. Instead, they say, the request for euthanasia may come from the patient's family, who may be tiring of the strain and expense of caring for an ill relative, or from physicians, who believe their expertise enables them to make that decision for the patient. Opponents claim that euthanasia could even be initiated by a bureaucracy that does not want the expense of providing terminal care.

Who Might Request Euthanasia?

Euthanasia deals with the quality of life and the quality of dying. People who request euthanasia often include those who feel their quality of life has shrunk to zero. They are no longer well enough to enjoy life or do the things they used to do. Other patients find the indignity of being cared for as if they were an infant too much to take.

Some want to die before they become very sick. Many patients suffering from serious diseases such as amytrophic lateral sclerosis (ALS, or Lou Gehrig's disease), Alzheimer's, multiple sclerosis, AIDS, and other illnesses seek the release of death before suffering the inevitable pain and decline of their conditions.

Dr. Harold Glucksberg told the story of one of his patients, a thirty-four-year-old man suffering from AIDS. He had been in severe pain for four months and was in danger of becoming blind. The patient asked for drugs to end his misery.

Dr. Glucksberg wanted to honor his request but was unable to because assisted suicide was against the law. The patient later committed suicide by jumping off a bridge. Dr. Glucksberg said he believed that the man must have been aided by close family members because he was in too weakened a condition to have done it by himself.[4]

A Complicated Issue

The rights an individual can expect in regard to his or her own death are legal as well as moral issues. Scientific advances have provided us with options never before available. Exploring those options forces us to face new questions.

Euthanasia is a very complicated and emotionally charged issue. And it is a subject many people prefer not to face. However, many people will have to face it at some point—if not for themselves, then when a loved one who is seriously ill desires a "good death."

Chapter 2

Historical Viewpoints

Historical views on suicide greatly influence beliefs about euthanasia today. Christians the world over have been opposed to suicide for centuries. They believe it goes against the sixth commandment, "Thou shalt not kill." (However, some argue that the commandment, literally translated, means, "Thou shalt not commit murder.")[1]

Saint Augustine (A.D. 354–430) was the first to condemn suicide as going against God's word. He had a tremendous impact on public opinion. Saint Thomas Aquinas (1225–1274) went even further in his declarations against suicide. He proclaimed it was a mortal sin, contrary to natural law, damaging to the community, and a symbol of humans involving themselves in what was a divine decision. His beliefs became a part of the Christian religion, particularly the Roman Catholic Church.

Religious Beliefs

The Catholic Church's condemnation of suicide is very strong. As a matter of fact, for centuries the

Catholic clergy refused funeral rites and burial in consecrated ground to those who committed suicide. They were buried in a separate area without the blessings of the Church. In modern times that has changed. Although the Church is still against suicide, it has come to believe that blame cannot be placed solely on the individual but can also be attributed to the pressures of modern society.

The Vatican is the seat of the Roman Catholic Church. Its decisions influence more than one billion Catholics. The Vatican's Declaration of 1980 affirms the Church's position against suicide and euthanasia: "Intentionally causing one's own death, or suicide, is . . . equally as wrong as murder; such an action . . . is to be considered as a rejection of God's sovereignty and loving plan."[2] The Catholic Church believes that we have no right to end our lives or the lives of others, a position with which the Greek Orthodox Church agrees. Many Protestants, however, such as Episcopalians, Methodists, Presbyterians, and Quakers, are more accepting of euthanasia, believing it is a matter of individual choice.

The Islamic religion is against both active and passive euthanasia. The

*T*he Catholic Church is strongly against euthanasia, believing it to be murder. Above, people who oppose euthanasia pray outside a hospital. The husband of a comatose patient in the hospital has petitioned a court to have her feeding tube removed.

holy book of Islam, the Koran, states: "Take not life which Allah [God] made sacred otherwise than in the course of justice." According to Muslim scholars, "The concept of a life not worthy of living does not exist in Islam."[3]

Hindu teachings are similar. Dr. T. P. Mishra, an expert in Hindu scriptures, says it is "clearly stated that the soul has to undergo all pleasures and pains allotted to a body in which it resides."[4]

Orthodox Jews are against active euthanasia. In 1997, they issued a statement declaring, "We believe that the recognition of a constitutionally recognized right to die for the terminally ill is a clear statement against the recognition and sanctity of human life."[5]

There are many other religious groups. Most have issued some kind of statement defining their beliefs on suicide and euthanasia hoping to help guide their followers. Some people follow such guidance strictly. For others, personal experiences may cause them to question their religious beliefs.

Modern Viewpoints

Whatever religious teachings an individual follows, it is clear that some people feel they have lost control over their own deaths. They believe that although death may have occurred naturally in the past, medical science now forces some to endure painful, debilitating illnesses and slower deaths.

There are more elderly people than ever before. For some of them, advances in medicine mean that they will live longer but will be in worse health. As life spans lengthen, the chances increase for people to experience pain, illness, and dementia (mental deterioration). Polls throughout the world and the

United States indicate a growing demand for the legal aspects of euthanasia to be addressed.

This demand did not occur overnight. The topic has been debated for over a century. In 1891, the Supreme Court stated: "No right is more sacred, or is more carefully guarded, by the common law, than the right of the individual to the possession and control of his own person."[6] Some feel this statement logically leads to the conclusion that a person should have control of his or her own death if that is what he or she wishes.

The Fight for Active Euthanasia

During the 1930s, the Euthanasia Society of America was formed in the United States. It was the first group in the country specifically dedicated to bringing the issue out in the open.[7]

Another group advocating euthanasia is the Hemlock Society. It was formed by Derek Humphry in 1980. One of the strongest and most vocal groups, it has more than 27,000 members across the United States. The Hemlock Society works to change legislation in favor of euthanasia. It also produces many publications about the subject in an effort to educate the public. The Hemlock Society offers support for people contemplating euthanasia.[8]

Many people who support euthanasia do not only believe they should have the right to request lethal drugs. They also feel that doctors should help them take the drugs if asked to do so. Although this is illegal in the United States (except in Oregon), there are many cases where physicians have agreed to help patients. Most of the time this is done secretly, and the doctors are not prosecuted.

The Nazi Euthanasia Program

Under the guise of euthanasia, a program of murder took place in Germany from December 1939 to August 1941. Between fifty thousand and sixty thousand physically and mentally handicapped adults were killed either by poison gas or lethal injection.

It is suspected that about five thousand severely disabled children were also put to death. The German people were told that a special program for children called "Kinderfachabteil" was being established all over the country. Parents were told their children were being sent to intensive care units where advanced medical experiments could help them recover.

After the child's death, a letter was sent home to the parents stating that the child had died unexpectedly. The letters said,

> The life of the deceased had been a torment to him/her on account of his/her severe mental trouble. You should therefore feel that his/her death was a happy release.

It then asked where to send the ashes of the deceased, as all bodies were cremated.[9]

These horrible murders linked to the term euthanasia caused many people to be opposed to the concept under any circumstances.

The Hemlock Society

Derek Humphry lived in England with his wife, Jean, a cancer patient who decided to take her own life. Derek helped her by preparing a lethal combination of drugs and giving them to her on a date they had agreed upon. After her death, he was questioned by authorities but was not charged because of lack of evidence. He later wrote about this experience in a book titled *Jean's Way*.

He moved to the United States and founded the Hemlock Society in 1980. It became a very influential group and membership grew rapidly. The Hemlock Society advocates both active and passive euthanasia. In 1991, Derek Humphry wrote his most famous book, *Final Exit*. This book basically told people how to commit suicide if they wished. It has become a national best-seller, selling over half a million copies.[10]

Shown below, Humphry debates Dr. Ira Byock, an opponent of assisted suicide.

Derek Humphry   Ira Byock, M.D.

Snowing

One common way of accomplishing euthanasia without detection is through a practice known among medical personnel as "snowing." Snowing involves giving the patient enough morphine to shut down the respiratory system, causing death.

Pain relief is an essential part of treating terminally ill patients, and morphine is often used in large doses for pain relief. This can have the double effect of relieving pain and causing death to occur sooner than it would naturally. It has been argued that the benefit of pain relief outweighs the ill effect of hastened death.[11]

Doctors' Views

Many doctors support physician-assisted suicide. A study of 1,902 doctors conducted by Dr. Diane Meier of Mount Sinai School of Medicine in New York reported that 6.4 percent of physicians surveyed admitted that they had helped at least one patient commit suicide. It went on to say that "requests for assisted suicide or euthanasia are frequently made to physicians who practice in specialties in which they are likely to care for dying patients, and that the decision to honor such a request is not rare in the United States."[12]

Other doctors, while not advocating physician-assisted suicide, do believe that prolonging life is not appropriate in some circumstances. In an anonymous survey taken to gauge physicians' responses on how far medicine should go to save a life, one doctor stated, "I do not think a patient's life should be prolonged just to prolong life. Heroic measures [extraordinary medical treatments] are simply not rational or humane."[13]

Oregon's Death with Dignity Act

According to Oregon law, in order for a patient to receive lethal drugs from a physician, specific guidelines must be followed:

- The patient must be an Oregon resident, at least eighteen years old, who has been diagnosed with a terminal illness that will lead to death within six months.

- The patient must make two oral requests to a physician for assistance in dying, separated by at least fifteen days.

- The patient must give the physician a signed, written request that has been witnessed by two persons, one not a relative of the patient.

- A second physician must be consulted; the second physician must confirm the patient's diagnosis and prognosis.

- Both physicians must determine that the patient is competent and is acting voluntarily.

- The physician must inform the patient of alternatives to assisted suicide, such as comfort care, pain control, and hospice care.

- If the patient is found to be mentally or emotionally distressed, he or she must be referred for a psychological examination.

- The physician must request that the patient's next of kin be notified, and the patient notified that he or she can change the decision at any time.

To comply with the law, physicians must report all prescriptions for lethal medication to the Oregon Health Division. Physicians are not obligated to participate in the Death with Dignity Act.[14]

Another doctor said, "One does not try heroics on ninety-nine-year-old patients, but does pull out all the stops on children and young adults."[15]

This raises some interesting points. Should age be a factor when determining the extent of medical care? What if the patient is considered to be of no particular importance to society? What if the patient is a criminal? What if the patient has no money to pay for care? Should the quality of life be a deciding factor? Who should judge what quality of life is acceptable?

Most people would agree that everyone has the right to choose to live. The right to die remains an unanswered question. Many groups, religious organizations, and medical and legal professionals are involved in addressing the problem of euthanasia. Centuries of personal beliefs, accepted norms of society, and legal precedents influence what is happening today.

Chapter 3

Terms and Concepts

The terms and concepts of euthanasia can be very confusing. Upon hearing the word euthanasia, many automatically assume it means putting someone "to sleep"—in other words, intentionally causing death. This is only one type of euthanasia. Intentionally causing death refers only to active euthanasia, or causing a person's death to occur quicker than it normally would. Active euthanasia is debated in hospitals and courts all over the world today.

Passive euthanasia, although more accepted than active euthanasia, is still very controversial. Passive euthanasia is accomplished by discontinuing or not offering lifesaving measures to a critically ill person. Such measures are often referred to as "heroic measures." They include cardiopulmonary resuscitation (CPR), the use of a respirator, and tube feeding. CPR is used for a patient whose heart or breathing has stopped; a respirator provides oxygen and breathes for a patient; and tube feeding involves placing a tube in the stomach to provide nourishment to patients who cannot eat by themselves.

Patients who are on respirators and being tube fed are often coma and PVS patients.

PVS Patients

PVS means "persistent vegetative state." In crude terms, these patients used to be referred to as vegetables. While many coma patients do eventually recover, PVS patients are believed to be in deep comas with no probable hope for recovery or regaining consciousness.

The medical community recognizes two types of death. Normally, a person's heart stops, the body shuts down, and death occurs within minutes. But in cases of severe illness or injury, the cerebral cortex, the "thinking" part of the brain, may shut down while the brain stem, which controls such things as breathing, blood pressure, and heart rate, continues to work. While in this type of coma, patients cannot hear, speak, eat, or respond to any stimuli. They are bedridden and often hooked to machines that keep them alive. This condition can continue for years as long as their machines continue to provide oxygen, if necessary, and nourishment.

According to *The Guinness Book of World Records*, the patient who remained comatose the longest ever was Elaine Esposito. She went into a coma after surgery in 1941 and remained that way for thirty-seven years until her death in 1978.[1]

PVS cases are heartbreaking for family members. Seeing their loved ones alive yet unable to respond to anything is devastating. Many people feel it would be better to simply disconnect the machines and allow the patient to die. And many feel that if they were to be in that situation, they would not want to continue living.

The Controversy Over Artificial Nutrition

Artificial nutrition and hydration, also known as tube feeding, were first developed only as a means of helping a person overcome a temporary inability to eat or swallow water—for example, as part of the recovery process after an operation. The practice of using artificial nutrition and hydration became widespread in the 1970s. Now it is routinely used on PVS patients. Those for euthanasia argue that the inability to eat and lack of appetite are natural symptoms of a dying body. They do not feel artificial nutrition should always be used. In the past, a patient unable to eat would not be considered to be starving to death but merely showing common symptoms of dying.[2]

Denying food and oxygen by machines to patients who are PVS or otherwise very ill can cause conflict. Family members sometimes disagree with the experts' decision. These conflicts can turn into legal battles involving the courts.

Advance Directives

There are now some legal ways to protect one's wishes before illness strikes. These are known as advance directives. They are legal papers people can sign stating the treatment they wish to receive if they are unable to speak for themselves. Advance directives are legally binding, that is, doctors and hospitals are required to abide by them.

One form of advance directive is a DNR order. DNR means "do not resuscitate." This indicates that a patient does not want to be resuscitated should his or her heart or breathing stop. This may occur during surgery or a serious illness. For example, cancer patients, patients with failing kidneys, or AIDS patients might sign a DNR order.

If a person wishes to be allowed to die if his or her heart or breathing stops, a DNR order must be on file. DNR orders are often included with other administrative papers to be signed upon admission to the hospital. DNR orders are strictly voluntary. It is very important for people to be informed before they agree to sign any papers.

Another useful form one might consider signing in advance is a durable power of attorney, or DPA. A DPA designates a trusted friend or family member to make medical decisions for the person who signs it. A DPA goes into force when a person is unconscious or otherwise unable to make such decisions. With a DPA, a person is essentially putting his or her life into the hands of another, so trust and sharing of one's wishes before a medical crisis occurs is very important.

Living Wills

Possibly the most well known and controversial type of advance directive is known as a living will. Living wills come into effect when a person is terminally ill, generally having less than six months to live. In a living will, the person who signs it describes in advance the type of medical treatment he or she wishes to receive or does not wish to receive, such as not being tube fed or hooked to a respirator. A living will ensures that a person's life will not be prolonged artificially during the final stages of a terminal illness. Living wills are recognized by every state in the United States. Both living wills and DPAs can be revoked at any time if a person changes his or her mind.

The concept of living wills was first introduced to the public in the late 1960s by the Euthanasia Education Council. Believing that every person has a right to choose not to have medical care, members of the council prepared and distributed formal requests for patients to sign. These forms stated:

> If there is no reasonable expectation of my recovery from physical or mental disability, I, _____, request that I be allowed to die and not be kept alive by artificial means or heroic measures.[3]

When the popular newspaper column "Dear Abby" ran an article describing the document, 50,000 people sent in requests for copies. By 1975, the Euthanasia Education Council had mailed out over 750,000 copies.[4]

In 1976, California was the first state to pass legislation legally recognizing living wills. This legislation was known as the Natural Death Act. Assemblyman Barry Keene, who introduced the bill, said he felt that it was the result of a generation's "searching for ways to rehumanize the dying process, and the product of a generation which views with horror the confrontation between modern technology and the human needs of dying."[5]

Living wills are very useful in helping family members cope during difficult times. Without a living will, crucial decisions have to be made by loved ones under extreme emotional strain. People who want living wills must take care to see that they are properly executed, since laws can vary from state to state.

Opposition to Living Wills

Some people are opposed to living wills. They think living wills can be abused by family members who are not willing to spend money or effort to help their ill relatives.

Some doctors are not in favor of living wills, feeling that they should make the decision as to what is reasonable treatment. In addition, they say that it is already standard practice to stop treatment if it has no chance of helping the patient. Some people in

*A*dvance directives, such as living wills and durable powers of attorney, allow people to make their wishes known before they become ill. This can be very helpful to family members faced with difficult decisions.

the medical community fear that living wills could backfire, requiring them to administer lifesaving technology to all patients who have not signed them.

Others are opposed to living wills because they say it is difficult for people to predict their own desires. As a group of Canadian doctors noted:

> An advance directive prepared by a healthy person is not a valid indicator of the preferences of a similar person when sick. . . . Our experience is that people change their minds when they become unwell, but an earlier advance directive might still be in force.[6]

Hospice

Hospice is a special kind of care that attempts to offer a peaceful death to the terminally ill without euthanasia. It attempts to help keep patients out of the hospital, in their home or another comfortable environment. Close to 400,000 terminally ill people come under hospice care each year, and most of them die at home.[7] Hospice workers and medical professionals, often along with clergy members, work together to provide support for the family caring for a terminally ill patient. Medical treatment for the patient, medications and supplies, and home health aides are available through hospice programs. In addition, hospice programs provide patients and families with therapy and counseling, including bereavement counseling.

Chapter 4

Reasons for Euthanasia

Many people argue that the case for euthanasia becomes dramatically apparent when true-life stories are examined. One such story belongs to Karen Ann Quinlan, possibly the most famous coma patient of all. Her story made international headlines.

Karen was twenty-two years old when she attended a party on April 15, 1975. After drinking alcohol and possibly taking tranquilizers, Karen was found without a pulse. She was taken to Saint Clare's, a Catholic hospital in Denville, New Jersey, and placed on a respirator. Her condition quickly deteriorated. Within days, her body curled up into a fetal position and she was considered to be in a PVS state.

A month passed with no change, and her family asked that Karen be disconnected from the respirator and allowed to die. The hospital refused, stating that Karen was not competent to make that decision and that her parents could not make it on her behalf.

Karen's parents took their case to court. On March 31, 1976, after a long legal battle, the New

Jersey Supreme Court authorized Karen to be unhooked from the respirator, although she would continue to be tube fed. Two weeks after this date, however, Karen was still connected to the respirator. When Karen's father questioned the hospital as to why they were not abiding by the court's decision, he was told to be patient.

What Karen's parents did not know was that the staff at the hospital had anticipated the court's ruling and were in the process of weaning Karen off the respirator. They hoped that if they disconnected her for small amounts of time each day, her body would learn to breathe on its own. According to notes taken by hospital personnel at the time, the plan seemed to be working.

Karen's parents continued to wait for her to be totally disconnected. Sister Urban, the president of the Saint Clare's board of trustees, said, "You have to understand our position, Mr. Quinlan. In this hospital we don't kill people."

Joe Quinlan shouted, "We're not asking you to *kill* anyone!" His intention had always been to continue the tube feeding. During the trial he had stated, "Intravenous is food. You can't remove that. That would be euthanasia." To him there was a distinct difference between tube feeding and use of a respirator.[1]

*K*aren Ann Quinlan was twenty-two years old when she went into a persistent vegetative state. The question of whether her respirator should be disconnected went to the New Jersey Supreme Court.

Karen was eventually removed from the respirator and did continue to breathe on her own. She remained alive for years, although she never regained consciousness. Karen eventually contracted pneumonia and was not given antibiotics to fight it. She died in June 1985, ten years after becoming comatose. Her ordeal had finally ended.

The Case of Nancy Cruzan

Nancy Cruzan's case was similar to Karen's, with two distinct differences: Nancy had previously expressed her wishes that she would not want to live hooked up to machines, and her parents wanted to discontinue her tube feeding.

In 1983, twenty-five-year-old Nancy was in a horrible car crash. She veered off an icy road, hit trees and a mailbox, overturned her car, and was thrown thirty-five feet before landing facedown in a ditch. The paramedics who found her could detect no pulse and estimated that she had not been breathing for twelve minutes, possibly longer. They gave her CPR, and her breathing and heartbeat returned. She was rushed to a hospital, but she never regained consciousness.

During the heartbreaking time that followed, her father once mournfully remarked, "If only the ambulance had arrived five minutes earlier, or five minutes later."[2] As it was, her loved ones were forced to watch her lie in her bed, seemingly lifeless, hooked up to machines.

A year after the accident, Nancy's husband divorced her, and her parents became her legal guardians. In 1987, four years after the accident, the Cruzans asked that her feeding tube be removed. The nursing home taking care of Nancy refused. The

Cruzans went to court and began what was to become a lengthy legal battle. The Missouri court system bounced the case to the Supreme Court of the United States, which then sent the case back to Missouri. The Supreme Court's reasoning was that although they found that Nancy had a right to die, Missouri had the right to set legal requirements regarding evidence that the patient would want treatment ended.

The Cruzans went back to the Missouri court with new testimony supporting their contention that Nancy would not want to live as she was. Although she had not signed a living will, she had stated on various occasions that she would not want to live unless her life was at least somewhat normal. The Cruzans ultimately won their case.

After the tube was finally removed and Nancy lay dying, a group of people stormed the hospital. They were pro-life activists who were trying to get into Nancy's room to force-feed her. Nineteen people were jailed. In the end, however, Nancy died, twelve days after the feeding tube was removed.

The Cruzans issued a statement calling her "our bright flaming star who flew through the heavens of our lives."[3] On her tombstone they inscribed:

> Nancy Beth Cruzan, Most loved Daughter— Sister—Aunt—Born, July 20, 1957—Departed, January 11, 1983—At peace, December 26, 1990.[4]

Both the Quinlan case and the Cruzan case brought important questions concerning euthanasia to the attention of the public. One example is the argument as to whether or not artificial nutrition and hydration are basic care or heroic measures. Some argue that if tube feeding is simply another form of feeding a patient, then a respirator is simply another way of helping the patient breathe; both are essentially the same type of care. Like Karen, Nancy was able to function without a respirator. Would Nancy have also continued to live had only her respirator been turned off? Nancy was essentially starved to death. Although starvation is painful, it was surmised that she could no longer feel pain. Was the decision of the court correct? Those for euthanasia feel it was.

Dr. Barnard's Opinion of Euthanasia

The doctors and medical care workers in the Quinlan and Cruzan cases fought to continue the life of their patients. But not all doctors share the same feelings. Many are in favor of euthanasia.

Dr. Christiaan Barnard, a world-famous heart surgeon who died in 2001, was an advocate for euthanasia. He admitted, "I have never practiced active euthanasia for one reason only—it is illegal. But I have often stood at the bedside of a dying patient and realized the need for this service."[5]

In fact, when his own mother fell ill, Barnard made the decision not to prolong her life. He said,

> I gave instructions to the doctor attending my own mother in her last illness that she should receive no antibiotics nor be tube fed. At that stage, she was in her ninety-eighth year, suffering from her third stroke and unconscious with pneumonia.
>
> I am convinced that is what she wanted. During the eleven years after her first stroke, as she lay bedridden with repeated bladder and lung infections, she told me on occasion, "I wish God would come and take me away."[6]

Isobel's Story

Mrs. Isobel Lejeune, an eighty-nine-year-old woman, was sitting in her garden watching the birds when she suddenly collapsed into a coma. Her family thought she had died. Although they were very sad, they were also glad her death had come swiftly and she had been spared any pain. But the doctor discovered Lejeune was still breathing and rushed her to the hospital. Her family expected her to slip away during the night. But the doctors kept her alive for the next three years.

Her daughter described Lejeune's sad condition:

> She was more or less unconscious, but never again coherent, or able to recognize us without confusion. She was incontinent; she had to be fed. They could not keep her in bed without bars.

The family was often called to come immediately because she had fallen and was suffering from severe bruising. Three times she broke an arm, and one time she broke her hip. When the family visited her, many times they found her bewildered and unhappy, with tears running down her face.

After her death, the family donated money to a euthanasia group. Lejeune's daughter told them why:

> We despise a system that can inflict such mental and physical pain. This experience has changed our whole outlook. We dread to find ourselves in the power of such people. Please continue your efforts for the sake of the dignity of ordinary decent people.[7]

Dr. Jack Kevorkian

Dr. Jack Kevorkian has been the most vocal and active supporter of euthanasia in our time. He not only supports it, he practices it. He is known as "Dr. Death" and has personally assisted in more than 130 suicides. He invented a "suicide machine" consisting of an intravenous tube connected to three bottles in a frame: one holding harmless saline solution; one with thiopental, a barbiturate that causes unconsciousness; and a third with the poison potassium chloride.

*D*r. Jack Kevorkian, shown here with one of his "suicide machines," is an outspoken advocate of euthanasia. He has personally assisted in more than 130 suicides and has gone to jail for breaking the law.

One of Dr. Kevorkian's patients was Janet Adkins, a fifty-four-year-old Oregon woman with Alzheimer's disease. Adkins's physician felt she had possibly three or four more good years left before the dementia of Alzheimer's disease took hold. However, Adkins decided she did not want to put her family or herself through that experience. She contacted Dr. Kevorkian and asked him for help.

On June 4, 1990, Adkins went with Dr. Kevorkian to a public park outside of Detroit, Michigan. As she reclined in the back of a VW camper, Kevorkian hooked her up to the intravenous tube, and the saline solution began to flow into her body. Janet herself pressed the button to release the thiopental and potassium chloride, murmuring, "Thank you, thank you." Kevorkian replied, "Have a nice trip." Six minutes later, her heart stopped beating.[8]

Kevorkian was charged with murder, but the case was later dismissed. In 1991, he assisted in three more suicides and the state of Michigan revoked his license to practice medicine. But he continued to assist in many suicides. The attention he brought to the issue of euthanasia had an impact in his home state of Michigan. Legislation was proposed to legalize physician-assisted suicide for the terminally ill, but in November 1998, the voters ultimately rejected it.

Oregon Law

Regardless of his personal beliefs, Dr. Kevorkian went to jail for breaking the law. Had he been a resident of the state of Oregon, his story may have had a different outcome. Oregon is the only state with a specific law permitting physician-assisted suicide. In that state a doctor can legally prescribe lethal

Oregon: The First Two Years

Oregon's "Death with Dignity Act" went into effect in 1997. According to the 2000 annual report, thirty-nine prescriptions for lethal doses of medication were written during that year. This figure shows a very slight rise in requests: In 1999, thirty-three requests were made, and in 1998, twenty-four were made.

These patients were very similar to other patients in Oregon who died naturally of their diseases, except that they were more likely to have a college education. Along with other concerns, these patients expressed their worry about becoming a burden to their families.

The report shows that physicians were in attendance at 52 percent of the reported deaths. However, the law provides for no regulatory authority to monitor the assisted suicides and no penalties for doctors who do not report prescribing lethal doses.[9]

drugs intended to kill a patient. These drugs are even covered by some Oregon health-insurance programs.

It is estimated that dozens of patients have been euthanized in Oregon, following the state's guidelines. But the fight for euthanasia has barely begun. In almost every state there are lawmakers who are proposing laws to allow physician-assisted suicide.

Chapter 5

Reasons Against Euthanasia

Most people who are opposed to euthanasia personally find it immoral, believing that killing, even killing oneself, is a sin. In addition, some people fear that if human life becomes devalued, some terminal patients might be deemed worthless and their relatives or health-care providers might push to euthanize them rather than continue to care for them. Advocates for the disabled claim that endorsing euthanasia implies that the lives of disabled people are not worth living.

Anti-euthanasia advocates also argue that believing a patient's disease or condition to be incurable is unnecessarily negative, because a cure could be found at any time. They also cite cases of patients who were believed to be dying but who subsequently recovered.

Many people fear that economics will also play a part in euthanasia. Lethal drugs used for this purpose cost around $35–$50.[1] Continued medical care and pain control medication can cost thousands of dollars. Often, doctors and hospitals are only reimbursed a limited amount by insurance companies.

Misdiagnosed PVS Cases

Opponents of euthanasia often argue that patients diagnosed as being in a persistent vegetative state can and do recover, or at least regain some of their abilities. Therefore, they say, withdrawing life support is wrong. A study published in July 1996 in the *British Medical Journal* seems to back these claims.

The study involved severely disabled patients presumed to be incapable of thinking, communicating, or sensing their surroundings. Of the forty patients diagnosed as being in PVS, seventeen (43 percent) were later found to have been misdiagnosed: They were alert and aware. The authors wrote:

> All patients remained severely physically disabled, but nearly all were able to communicate their preference in quality of life issues, some at a high level.[2]

Would doctors conveniently eliminate terminal patients once these limits are met? While this idea may seem extreme, many claim that people on public assistance and programs such as Medicaid already receive substandard medical care. Attorney and consumer advocate Wesley Smith believes, "The last people to receive medical care will be the first to receive assisted suicide."[3]

Many people also believe that those requesting euthanasia often do so because they are depressed, because they are in pain, or because they cannot take care of themselves and do not want to burden their families. Providing these people with counseling, adequate pain medication, and hospice care might mean they would change their minds about euthanasia.

Disabled People Speak Out

Lisa K. Gigliotti was a college student who was used to running three miles daily when she was stricken with rheumatoid arthritis and had to be taken care of at home. Her memories of that time are grim:

> I was totally incapacitated. I needed someone to lift my head and hold a glass for me to drink, and I needed to use a bedpan and had to be cleaned.[4]

Her mother and grandmother were later killed in an automobile accident. With no one to care for her, Lisa was admitted to a nursing home. Her experience was horrible. Her roommate was a PVS patient. The nurses were impatient, rude, and sometimes could not speak English. Lisa remembers having to wait forty-five minutes for a bedpan. She says, "Even the strongest of human psyches is affected when treated as a burden rather than treated with dignity."[5] Lisa feels people sometimes want euthanasia because they fear their own impending helplessness. If they had better care and understanding, they might not want to die.

Lisa fought severe depression and learned to become independent with the use of a wheelchair. She became an attorney and policy advisor for the Michigan Senate. She lends her voice to those against euthanasia. Her own situation taught her to fight against all odds and never give up hope.

Robert C. Horn III, a professor and author from California State University, is suffering with Lou Gehrig's disease and has severe loss of voluntary

*M*any disabled people are strong opponents of euthanasia because they feel it implies that their lives are not worth living and because they fear that they will be pressured to commit suicide. Here a group of disabled activists demonstrates against euthanasia.

muscle control. Many would judge his quality of life to be poor or even nonexistent. But Mr. Horn fights to continue living. He explains his reasons:

> After five years of being tethered to a ventilator [respirator], "eating" via a tube in my stomach, "talking" with my eyebrows and operating the computer with my foot, did I make the right choice? You bet! What I have left is more valuable than what I have lost. The things I can do are more important than those I can't. . . . I can think, reason and analyze, remember, read, write, learn and communicate. I can love, feel happiness and sadness, be enthusiastic, get angry, feel joy. I can believe, hope and have faith."[6]

Unexpected Recoveries of PVS Patients

The case against euthanasia is also strongly supported by stories of unexpected recoveries of patients who were believed to be in a persistent vegetative state. Doctors thought that Carol Dusold, a nineteen-year-old woman who was involved in an accident that broke her left arm and severely bruised her brain stem, would not recover. She was in a deep coma. Her body twisted up and she wasted away to sixty-five pounds. The doctors told her mother that all they could do "is try to starve her by taking the intravenous out." Her mother, a devout Lutheran, refused, and began a four-month vigil beside Carol's bed. She talked to her constantly and let her know she loved her. Carol recovered, married, and had a child. She has only a slight limp, a small speech impediment, and a damaged left hand. Doctors were amazed at her recovery.[7]

Pain Management

Proper pain management is essential to quality of life for terminally ill patients. Opponents of euthanasia argue that many people who request euthanasia would not do so if their pain were managed adequately. Several factors can interfere with people getting the pain medication they need, including:

- Reluctance to report pain
- Concern about distracting physicians from treatment of the underlying disease
- Fear that pain means the disease is worse
- Concern about not being a "good" patient
- Reluctance to take pain medications
- Fear of addiction or being thought of as an addict
- Worries about unmanageable side effects
- Concern about becoming tolerant to pain medications[8]

Misuse of Advance Directives

Anti-euthanasia advocates also say that advance directives can be misused. People can sign advance directives when they are healthy, then later change their minds about the extent of the care they wish to receive. Or they can sign a directive without understanding its implications. Ill or injured people could even sign them because of pressure from relatives or medical staff. For example, Joe Ehman, a news reporter from Rochester, New York, who uses a wheelchair, said he was "literally hounded" by social workers to sign a DNR order when he was hospitalized for back surgery in 1995. He cannot say for certain this was because of his disability but suspects that may have had something to do with the continual requests. A social worker even accosted him a few hours after surgery. Joe remembers the incident:

> Still delirious from the anesthesia and from post-surgical morphine and demerol, I had to hear from yet another social worker who wanted to force-feed me a DNR. I mustered my strength and screamed, "I'm 30 years old. I don't want to die!"[9]

Hospice As an Alternative

People opposed to euthanasia claim that the reason many patients want euthanasia is that they do not have adequate care and pain relief. One alternative to euthanasia is hospice care. Hospice care offers terminal patients and their families understanding and support that helps them through their difficult problems.

Dying at home in the care of relatives is certainly not a new idea; this is how people have died for centuries. However, as a modern alternative to hospital care, the hospice system was first founded in England by a physician, Dame Cicely Saunders, in 1967. The first American hospice was established in Connecticut in 1974. Originally, hospices were small hospitals dedicated to the care of terminal patients. Now the trend in the United States is for hospice care to take place in the home, with family members and other loved ones actively involved. Patients receive medication and care to keep them

Richard Lewis's Death

The family of Richard Lewis decided to use hospice care when Richard was dying from lung cancer. The hospice program provided physical and emotional support for Richard as well as support and therapy for his wife, Cheryl, and their two children, a twelve-year-old daughter and seven-year-old son. Richard was afraid to tell his children that he was dying, but Cheryl felt they already knew but were afraid to ask. After a conversation finally occurred, Cheryl recalled her daughter's fears: "A lot of my daughter's questions were things like: 'Where will we live? Will we have money for food? Will we have to get rid of our pets?'" Richard and Cheryl prepared their children as best they could and tried to calm their fears.

Deciding how close the children should be to their father's actual death was difficult. When Richard went into a coma, Cheryl allowed the children to stand by his bedside to say good-bye.

> My daughter went in and held his hand and told him she loved him. My son ran into his own bedroom to cry, then came out and said, "I'm going to Katie's" and went down the road to his friend's to stay for a few hours. He made it clear he didn't want to be around. When he came home and said, "Where's Dad?" I said, "He went to heaven." He said, "OK."

Although it was heartbreaking, Cheryl feels the experience offered her children some kind of closure in their father's death.[10]

comfortable rather than to treat the disease. Hospice workers, including nurses, counselors, and clergy if requested, visit on a regular basis to help with care and offer support.

Patients often feel guilty that they are a burden to their family. The family's reactions greatly influence a patient's behavior and even their health. Hospice workers help those involved cope with the weariness, anger, sadness, and other emotions.

Kenneth Doka, a Lutheran minister, encourages families of terminally ill patients to become involved with hospice as soon as possible. He says:

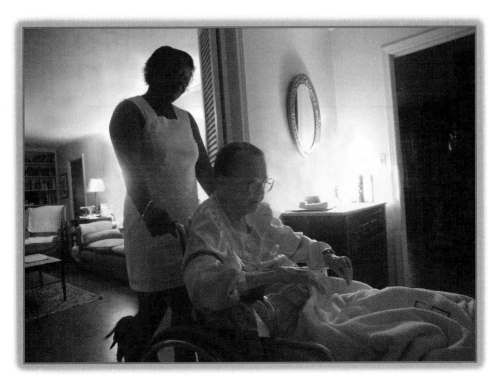

*H*ospice programs offer support and care for terminally ill people and their families, usually outside the hospital setting. Home health aides, nurses, counselors, and clergy visit on a regular basis.

This can help in the grieving process because having the knowledge that you were actively involved, the feeling that "we did what we could," can really be important in grief.[11]

The National Hospice Organization describes its philosophy:

Hospice affirms life. Hospice exists to provide support and care for persons in the last phases of incurable disease so that they might live as fully and comfortably as possible. Hospice recognizes dying as a normal process whether or not resulting from disease. Hospice neither hastens nor postpones death. Hospice exists in the hope and belief that, through appropriate care and the promotion of a caring community sensitive to their needs, patients and families may be free to attain a degree of mental and spiritual preparation for death that is satisfactory to them.[12]

Hospice, for some, is the best possible way to face death and have a dignified end surrounded by those they love. It is unfortunate there are not enough hospice programs available for the number of terminally ill patients who could benefit from them. If options such as hospice were more readily available, the question of euthanasia might not even arise.

Chapter 6

Questions Remain Unanswered

With supporters on both sides of the euthanasia issue fighting vigorously for their beliefs, it is unlikely that any resolution will be found quickly. Court battles are being waged constantly over individual cases. States are also reconsidering legislation that could have a huge impact on future practices regarding euthanasia.

Many polls indicate support of legalized euthanasia is not strong. One writer suggested that public opinion was split into thirds: a third of Americans support legalization under a wide variety of circumstances; a third support it in a few cases but oppose it in most; and a third oppose it under any circumstances.[1]

The Search for a Good Death Will Affect Many

The outcome of these legal battles, whatever it may be, will affect many. One study of people in North America concluded that "more often than not, patients died in pain, their desires concerning treatment neglected, after spending ten days or more in an intensive care unit."[2]

Another study estimated that of the 2 million Americans who die each year, nearly 85 percent die in an institution. Of those deaths, about 80 percent involve a decision as to whether or not to try to prolong life. Nearly four out of every five Americans die of a chronic, lingering illness.[3]

Suffering with no hope can be demeaning. Are we really prolonging life or merely delaying death? Devout religious believers insist euthanasia is a sin. But is it right to extend religious beliefs to the entire population? Is euthanasia to be considered a moral or legal issue? Is it possible to come to any satisfactory resolution if morals, ethics, and widely varying laws are all taken into consideration?

Care for the terminally ill and elderly is inadequate in many areas of the country. This is a huge issue that has a tremendous impact on the euthanasia question. Programs such as hospice, as well as proper counseling, are crucial to terminally ill patients. Should the government provide more funds to help in these areas?

The voices of the disabled continue to be raised against euthanasia. During a 1997 rally outside the Supreme Court building, more than two hundred protesters gathered to express their concerns. One disabled woman wore a badge that said, "Spare no expense. Keep me alive."[4] These people firmly believe if euthanasia is legalized, the disabled will be targeted to die as part of cost-cutting measures. Bob Liston, a disabled-rights advocate, believes the fears of the disabled need to be recognized. He said, "You can come up with lots of those heart-wrenching stories" about terminally ill people in terrible pain

*C*ourt battles are constantly being waged on both sides of the euthanasia issue. Shown is Andrew Batavia, a disabled attorney who argued for physician-assisted suicide in front of the Supreme Court.

who want help to die. "But they have to understand this isn't just about them."[5]

Education about advance directives is also needed. Is it the patient's responsibility to educate himself or herself in these matters? Should health care workers and physicians offer advice, or is that improper? If the patient seeks advice from his or her clergy or church, will all facts be presented fairly?

As current laws stand today, patients have limited control over their own deaths. And this control can easily be lost. Stories such as Nancy Cruzan's and Eli Kahn's emphasize the very real possibility that one's own desires will be ignored. Facing the prospect of dying is difficult. Many avoid even thinking about it. Yet considering the decisions one might have to make in advance and signing legal papers such as a living will might be the only defense against a long, drawn-out death. If these decisions are not made by the patients, others will make them. And they might easily make the wrong decision.

Doctors have declared many cases diagnosed as PVS to be hopeless when in fact the patients have recovered. In the case of Gary Stocks, a young man who was mugged and severely beaten, doctors said he would never be more than a vegetable. He remained paralyzed and in a coma for six weeks. But Gary recovered and at the age of twenty-six returned to college to continue his doctoral studies. His doctors proclaimed his recovery "unbeliev-able."[6] What if Gary had been euthanasized? Could such a situation occur? Those against euthanasia fear it could.

The complex issue of euthanasia is a part of society today and will probably remain so. The value of human life, its quality, and the inhumanity of suffering through terminal illnesses are factors being weighed in the modern debate about euthanasia. The question remains of when it is proper to forego medical science and let nature take its course, and whether or not to use medical science to hasten the inevitable ending. How should these questions be resolved? What do you think is right?

Organizations Opposed to Euthanasia

American Life League (ALL)
P.O. Box 1350
Stafford, VA 22555
(540) 659-4171

Center for the Rights of the Terminally Ill
P.O. Box 54246
Hurst, TX 76054-2064
(817) 656-5143

Human Life International (HLI)
4 Family Life
Front Royal, VA 22630
(540) 635-7884

National Right to Life Committee
419 Seventh Street NW, Suite 500
Washington, DC 20004-2293
(202) 626-8800

Organizations Supporting Euthanasia

Choice in Dying—The National Council for the Right to Die
1035 30th Street NW
Washington, DC 20007
(202) 338-9790

Compassion in Dying Federation
PMB415, 6312 SW
Capitol Highway
Portland, OR 97201
(503) 221-9556

Euthanasia Research and Guidance Organization (ERGO)
24829 Norris Lane
Junction City, OR 97448-9559
(541) 998-1873

The Hemlock Society
P.O. Box 101810
Denver, CO 80250-1810
(303) 639-1202
(800) 247-7421

Hospice Organizations

American Hospice Foundation
2120 L Street N.W., Suite 200
Washington, D.C. 20037
(202) 223-0204

National Hospice and Palliative Care Organization
1901 N. Moore Street, Suite 901
Arlington, VA 22209
(703) 243-5900
(800) 658-8898

Chapter 1. What Is a Good Death?

1. Dr. Christiaan Barnard, *Good Life, Good Death: A Doctor's Case for Euthanasia and Suicide* (Englewood Cliffs, N.J.: Prentice-Hall, Inc., 1980), p. 88.

2. Jerry B. Wilson, *Death by Decision: The Medical, Moral, and Legal Dilemmas of Euthanasia* (Philadelphia: Westminster Press, 1975), p. 57.

3. James Rachels, *The End of Life: Euthanasia and Morality* (Oxford, England: Oxford University Press, 1986), pp. 78–79.

4. Linda L. Emanuel, ed., *Regulating How We Die* (Cambridge, Mass.: Howard University Press, 1998), p. 204.

Chapter 2. Historical Viewpoints

1. Gerald A. Larue, *Euthanasia and Religion* (Los Angeles: The Hemlock Society, 1985), p. 3.

2. Sacred Congregation for the Doctrine of the Faith, "Declaration on Euthanasia," May 5, 1980, <http://www.vatican.va/roman_curia/congregations/cfaith/documents/rc_con_cfaith_doc_19800505_euthanasia_en.html> (September 14, 2001).

3. "Euthanasia and Physician Assisted Suicide: All Sides of the Issues," *Religious Tolerance Page*, n.d., <http://www.religioustolerance.org/euthanas.htm> (February 20, 2000).

4. Dr. Christiaan Barnard, *Good Life, Good Death: A Doctor's Case for Euthanasia and Suicide* (Englewood Cliffs, N.J.: Prentice-Hall, Inc., 1980), p. 91.

5. "Euthanasia and Physician Assisted Suicide: All Sides of the Issues."

6. Daniel Callahan, *The Troubled Dream of Life: Living With Mortality* (New York: Simon and Schuster, 1993), p. 103.

7. "U.S.A.," *The Voluntary Euthanasia Society Page*, n.d., <http://www.ves.org.uk/DpFS_USA.html> (May 31, 2001).

8. "Hemlock Services," *Hemlock Society Page*, n.d., <http://www.hemlock.org/hemlock> (May 10, 2000).

9. Robert N. Wennberg, *Terminal Choices: Euthanasia, Suicide, and the Right to Die* (Grand Rapids, Mich.: William B. Eerdman's Publishing Company, 1989), p. 214.

10. Brian P. Johnston, *Death as a Salesman: What's Wrong with Assisted Suicide* (Sacramento, Calif.: New Regency Publishing, 1998), p. 4.

11. Robin Peters, "Terms and Definitions," *Ethical Exits Page*, 2001, <http://www.ethicalexits.com/article1004.html> (May 31, 2001).

12. "Physician Assisted Suicide in the United States," *Religious Tolerance Page*, n.d., <http://www.religioustolerance.org/euth_us.htm> (July 19, 2001).

13. John Langone, *Thorny Issues* (Boston: Little, Brown and Company, 1981), p. 27.

14. "Oregon's Death with Dignity Act: Three Years of Legalized Physician-Assisted Suicide," *Oregon Health Division, Center for Health Statistics (and Vital Records) Page*, 2001, <www.ohd.hr.state.or.us/chs/pas/ar-intro.htm> (July 19, 2001).

15. Langone, p. 27.

Chapter 3. Terms and Concepts

1. *Guinness World Records 2000* (New York: Bantam Books, 2000), p. 262.

2. Daniel Callahan, *The Troubled Dream of Life: Living with Mortality* (New York: Simon and Schuster, 1993), p. 81.

3. Jerry B. Wilson, *Death by Decision: The Medical, Moral, and Legal Dilemmas of Euthanasia* (Philadelphia: Westminster Press, 1975), p. 41.

4. Peter G. Filene, *In the Arms of Others* (Chicago, Ill.: Ivan R. Dee, 1998), p. 98.

5. John Langone, *Thorny Issues* (Boston: Little, Brown and Company, 1981), p. 34.

6. Brian P. Johnston, *Death as a Salesman: What's Wrong with Assisted Suicide* (Sacramento, Calif.: New Regency Publishing, 1998), p. 168.

7. Suzanne Curley, "Surrounded by Love," *Newsday*, January 24, 1998, p. B1.

Chapter 4. Reasons for Euthanasia

1. Peter G. Filene, *In the Arms of Others* (Chicago: Ivan R. Dee, 1998), pp. 126, 132.

2. Ibid., p. 168.

3. "Death With Dignity FAQs," *Dying Well Network Page*, n.d., <http://www.bardo.org/DWD.html#One01> (August 14, 2001).

4. Filene, pp. 182–183.

5. Dr. Christiaan Barnard, *Good Life, Good Death: A Doctor's Case for Euthanasia and Suicide* (Englewood Cliffs, N.J.: Prentice-Hall, Inc., 1980), p. 77.

6. Ibid., p. 66.

7. Ibid., p. 100.

8. Filene, p. 188.

9. "Oregon's Death with Dignity Act: Annual Report 2000," *Oregon Health Division, Center for Health Statistics (and Vital Records) Page*, February 2001, <http://www.ohd.hr.state.or.us/chs/pas/ar-smmry.htm> (May 24, 2001).

Chapter 5. Reasons Against Euthanasia

1. Marilyn Golden, "Why Assisted Suicide Must Not Be Legalized," *Euthanasia Prevention Page*, n.d., <www.euthanasiaprevention.on.ca/Articles/whynot.htm> (August 10, 2001).

2. K. Andrews, L. Murphy, R. Munday, and C. Littlewood, "Misdiagnosis of the Vegetative State: Retrospective Study in a Rehabilitation Unit," *British Medical Journal*, vol. 313, 1996, pp. 13–16.

3. "Assisted Suicide and Cost Containment," *International Task Force on Euthanasia and Assisted Suicide Page*, Fall 1999, <http://www.iaetf.org/ascc.htm> (September 14, 2001).

4. John Bookser Feister, "Thou Shalt Not Kill: The Church Against Assisted Suicide," *Saint Anthony Messenger*, June 1997, <http:www.americancatholic.org/Messenger/Jun1997/feature1.asp> (July 19, 2001).

5. Ibid.

6. Robert C. Horn III, "Choosing Life, Even on a Ventilator," *Los Angeles Times*, May 16, 1996, p. D-9.

7. Gerald A. Larue, *Euthanasia and Religion* (Los Angeles: The Hemlock Society, 1985), p. 10.

8. Brian P. Johnston, *Death as a Salesman: What's Wrong with Assisted Suicide* (Sacramento, Calif.: New Regency Publishing, 1998), p. 37.

9. "Could You Please Die Now?" *RING! Online Page*, n.d., <http://199.190.91.5/nprofit/lifespan/die_now.htm> (August 14, 2001).

10. Suzanne Curley, "Surrounded by Love," *Newsday*, January 24, 1998, p. B1.

11. Ibid.

12. Derek Humphry and Ann Wickett, *The Right to Die: Understanding Euthanasia* (New York: Harper and Row, 1986), p. 183.

Chapter 6. Questions Remain Unanswered

1. Ezekiel Emanuel, "Whose Right to Die?" *Atlantic Monthly*, March 1997, <www.theatlantic. com/issues/97mar/emanuel/emanuel.htm> (May 31, 2000).

2. "Euthanasia and Physician Assisted Suicide: All Sides of the Issues," *Religious Tolerance Page*, n.d., <http://www.religioustolerance.org/euthanas. htm> (February 20, 2000).

3. "Death With Dignity FAQs," *Dying Well Network Page*, n.d., <http://www.bardo.org/DWD. html#One01> (August 14, 2001).

4. Lori Montgomery, "Outside court, disabled urge: 'Keep me alive.'" *Detroit Free Press*, January 9, 1997, <http://www.freep.com/news/extra2/qcrowd9. htm> (May 31, 2000).

5. Ibid.

6. Gerald A. Larue, *Euthanasia and Religion* (Los Angeles: The Hemlock Society, 1985), p. 10.

advance directive—A legal document stating what kind of care a patient desires should he or she become unable to make medical decisions.

AIDS (acquired immune deficiency syndrome)—An incurable condition in which a virus (HIV) weakens the body's natural defense system, leaving the body open to infection by potentially fatal diseases.

Alzheimer's disease—A progressive brain disease that causes loss of mental abilities.

appeal—To take steps to have a case heard in a higher court.

assisted suicide—A form of euthanasia in which a person is given access to the means to kill himself or herself by a doctor or other person.

CPR (cardiopulmonary resuscitation)—Technique used to restart a patient's heart or breathing.

dementia—Mental deterioration, a condition often found in the final stages of Alzheimer's disease.

DNR order (Do Not Resuscitate order)—An advance directive indicating that there should be no attempt to restart the patient's heart or restore breathing through CPR or any other lifesaving methods.

DPA (durable power of attorney)—An advance directive giving another person power to make medical decisions for a patient who is unable to do so.

euthanasia—The act of ending a person's life painlessly, usually to relieve incurable suffering.

heroic measures—Lifesaving methods such as CPR, use of respirator, and tube feeding.

hospice—A small hospital or home situation dedicated to caring for the terminally ill, including providing pain relief.

injection—Method of giving drugs by needle and syringe.

intravenous—Refers to giving medicine by needle to the veins.

living will—An advance directive that describes how a person would wish to be treated by doctors or caregivers if he or she became mentally or physically unable to make decisions.

Medicaid—A program of financial assistance for medical care for those unable to afford it, which is financed by state and federal government.

palliative care—The treatment of pain.

passive euthanasia—Withdrawal of medical treatment or life support resulting in a patient's death.

PVS (persistent vegetative state)—A deep coma, caused by brain damage, from which most patients do not recover.

respirator—A device for giving artificial respiration, also commonly called a ventilator.

snowing—Giving a patient a large dose of morphine, causing death.

suicide—Killing oneself intentionally.

voluntary euthanasia—Giving a severely ill patient, at his or her request, a lethal substance to end his or her life.

Books

Altman, Linda Jacobs. *Death: An Introduction to Medical-Ethical Dilemmas.* Berkeley Heights, N.J.: Enslow Publishers, 2000.

Boyd, Sunni. *Euthanasia.* San Diego, Calif.: Lucent Books, 1995.

Cavan, Seamus, and Sean Dolan. *Euthanasia: Debate Over the Right to Die.* New York: Rosen Publishing, 2000.

Egendorf, Laura K., editor. *Assisted Suicide.* San Diego, Calif.: Greenhaven Press, 2000.

Gay, Kathlyn. *The Right to Die: Public Controversy, Private Matter.* Brookfield, Conn.: Millbrook Press, 1993.

Torr, James D. *Euthanasia.* San Diego, Calif.: Greenhaven Press, 1999.

Walker, Richard. *A Right to Die?* Danbury, Conn.: Franklin Watts, 1997.

Winters, Paul A., editor. *Death and Dying: Opposing Viewpoints.* San Diego, Calif.: Greenhaven Press, 1998.

Yount, Lisa. *Physician-Assisted Suicide and Euthanasia.* New York: Facts on File, 2000.

Internet Addresses

The Hemlock Society
<http://www.hemlock.org>

National Right to Life Committee
<http://www.nrlc.org>

National Hospice and Palliative Care Organization
<http://www.nhpco.org>

Further Reading

Index